SUPERVISING PART-TIME EMPLOYEES

A Guide to Better Productivity

Elwood N. Chapman

A FIFTY-MINUTE™ SERIES BOOK

CRISP PUBLICATIONS, INC.
Menlo Park, California

SUPERVISING PART-TIME EMPLOYEES
A Guide to Better Productivity

Elwood N. Chapman

CREDITS:
Editor: **Follin Armfield**
Typesetting: **ExecuStaff**
Cover Design: **Carol Harris**
Artwork: **Ralph Mapson**

Copyright © 1994 Crisp Publications
Printed in the United States of America.

Distribution to the U.S. Trade:

National Book Network, Inc.
4720 Boston Way
Lanham, MD 20706
1-800-462-6420

Library of Congress Catalog Card Number 93-072501
Chapman, Elwood N.
Supervising Part-Time Employees
ISBN 1-56052-243-7

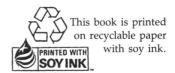

This book is printed on recyclable paper with soy ink.

PRINTED WITH SOY INK

LEARNING OBJECTIVES FOR:

SUPERVISING PART-TIME EMPLOYEES

The objectives for *Supervising Part-Time Employees* are listed below. They have been developed to guide you, the reader, to the core issues covered in this book.

Objectives

- ❏ **1) To explain why organizations should hire part-time workers.**

- ❏ **2) To discuss management considerations regarding hiring part-timers.**

- ❏ **3) To identify the characteristics of part-time workers.**

- ❏ **4) To explain special training needs of young and senior part-timers.**

Assessing Your Progress

In addition to the Learning Objectives, Crisp, Inc. has developed an **assessment** that covers the fundamental information presented in this book. A twenty-five item, multiple choice/true-false questionnaire allows the reader to evaluate his or her comprehension of the subject matter. An answer sheet with a summary matching the questions to the listed objectives is also available. To learn how to obtain a copy of this assessment please call: **1-800-442-7477** and ask to speak with a Customer Service Representative.

ABOUT THE AUTHOR

Elwood Chapman's self-help books have sold more than 2 million copies. He is well-known for his best-selling *Attitude, Your Most Priceless Possession, The New Supervisor, Comfort Zones,* and *Plan B: Converting Change Into Career Opportunity.*

A former professor of business at Chaffey College, "Chap," as he is known to his friends, has spent many years as a business consultant. He recently retired and spends much of his time "on the beach" writing self-help books.

ABOUT THE SERIES

With over 200 titles in print, the acclaimed Crisp 50-Minute™ series presents self-paced learning at its easiest and best. These comprehensive self-study books for business or personal use are filled with exercises, activities, assessments, and case studies that capture your interest and increase your understanding.

Other Crisp products, based on the 50-Minute books, are available in a variety of learning style formats for both individual and group study, including audio, video, CD-ROM, and computer-based training.

PREFACE

This book has been written primarily for supervisors. It is designed to assist them in gaining greater productivity from part-time personnel which, in turn, will lower labor costs. A secondary purpose is to assist management in their quest to better allocate and utilize human resources.

Questions answered in this publication include:

- Are there special techniques supervisors can use to get better results from younger, seasoned, and retired part-timers?

- Can full-timers who leave or retire be replaced with less expensive part-timers who can produce at a similar level?

- What are the advantages and disadvantages of hiring part-timers?

- Do high school and college part-timers require special handling if they are to produce at high levels?

- Can enthusiastic part-time employees motivate full-timers into higher productivity?

- Will flex-scheduling turn the future into the "decade of the part-timer"?

These and similar questions will be discussed. Given a chance, the policies recommended could give your organization the competitive edge it seeks—in both domestic and foreign markets.

A Special Note from the Author

All employees should be treated with the same degree of fairness and dignity regardless of their official status. This does not mean, however, that the supervisor should be insensitive to certain basic differences that may be present among part-timers due to the skills and experiences they may or may not possess.

In this book, part-timers have been divided by experience levels into *younger* employees, *experienced* workers, and *retirees*. The rationale is that each group requires special understanding if higher productivity is to be achieved.

For example, younger part-timers (those normally under the age of 25) have less work experience and a more narrow range of skills than do seasoned and retired part-timers. As a result, productivity is gained by creating an environment that provides a learning-transition period. Seasoned employees, on the other hand, can often add value to an organization because of past experience. Retirees often produce more when assigned special projects that require additional patience and insights.

Understanding the difference among the classifications—and the way to take advantage of them—can assist the supervisor in meeting the challenge of forming and maintaining an employee mix that will reach higher productivity and quality goals.

CONTENTS

P A R T

I

Changing to a
Part-Time Workforce

PART-TIMERS AS SUBSTITUTES FOR FULL-TIMERS

When we think of part-time employees, certain images usually come to mind: a food server working selected meals, a delivery courier who works after school, an office worker who does a specific task for two or four hours, three or four days a week, or someone who is hired to perform a limited function and may or may not require supervision.

This is the thinking of the past!

Today we must start thinking of part-timers as substitutes for full-timers. We must think of flexible scheduling—of people who can produce the same results in, say, three ten-hour days as current full-timers produce in the traditional forty-hour work week. Imagine the following:

- A part-time employee becoming an integral part of a work team even if she or he is present only fifteen hours a week.

- A production line that operates three days per week with only part-timers.

- A person who needs the income holding down two or three part-time jobs until he or she qualifies for a full-time position with full benefits.

- Two people sharing the same job on different shifts and producing much more than a single employee.

The era of the full-time employee with full benefits is under fire because of the escalating cost of health care and other benefits.* Also, the traditional eight-hour shift often produces only six hours of productivity. Two part-timers working four hours each might be able to produce more at substantially lower costs.

As long as these conditions persist and there is an available labor pool, part-timers will be in demand.

---

*The present administration in Washington is hoping to extend medical benefits to all Americans. The impact of possible new legislation requiring medical benefits for part-time employees is not known at this writing.

NEW STRATEGIES

Increasingly, both large and small companies are adopting the following strategies:

1. Managers will question every job to see if part-timers might do the same work at a lower cost.

2. When a vacancy results from the departure of a full-time employee, a part-time employee will be considered before another full-timer is employed.

3. Highly skilled employees who no longer want to work full-time may be offered the option of job-sharing.

4. Organizations will look at part-timers as interns or probationary employees who may become qualified to become full-timers in the future.

The purpose of this section is to raise questions and suggest avenues that an organization might take to discover its own best mix of full-time and part-time workers.

AVAILABILITY OF PART-TIMERS

The pool of people seeking part-time jobs has risen dramatically. A contracting economy, which has caused many organizations to reduce their employee base, combined with increasing numbers of women and retirees entering the work force, is largely responsible for this trend.

It is estimated that approximately one out of five current workers is a part-timer. Perhaps half of those would prefer full-time positions if they were available.

By the turn of the century, it is estimated that one out of every three workers may be part-time. Following are some considerations that help explain such a dramatic increase:

▶ More and more employers will focus on lowering their fixed costs. One way to do this is to reduce the size and make-up of the permanent work force.

▶ Specialization will increase, thus giving selected workers in high-demand industries the opportunity to earn high incomes from part-time positions.

▶ Flexible scheduling (flex-scheduling)—when employees start and finish a workday at different times—offers organizations an excellent way to cover early and/or late shifts.

▶ The pool of available students will remain high as they compete for the best part-time jobs to help cover increasing educational costs. In some cases, graduates unable to find full-time positions will hold down two or more part-time jobs.

▶ More parents are choosing to spend additional time with their children, and thus are seeking part-time work. Already, young couples have figured out that if one spouse works full-time (with benefits that cover the entire family), the other can work part-time on a flex-schedule and spend extra time at home.

▶ Retirees currently are actively seeking more part-time involvement. This figure will increase if inflation grows and/or retirement pensions shrink.

▶ Moonlighting will continue. Even with unemployment high, many people who already have full-time jobs seek additional income, and thus hold down "after-work," part-time positions.

WHAT IS A PART-TIMER?

Federal legislation defines a part-timer as a person who works less than 1,000 hours per year ($17\frac{1}{2}$ hours per week). The working world, however, generally sees a part-timer as an individual who works thirty hours per week or less, averaging about twenty.

Part-timers are divided into two basic groups: those who prefer to work part-time for their own reasons, and those who cannot find regular, full-time employment.

Normally those who prefer part-time work have a primary focus other than employment—for example, a college student taking a full load of courses or a parent who does not wish to be away from home for extended periods.

Those unable to find full-time employment usually seek and hold part-time jobs on a long-term temporary basis. Some accept "on-call" employment where the hours actually worked can range from one to seventy hours per week.

Part-time jobs usually, but not always, have these characteristics:

- Wages are typically lower.

- Only the basic or required benefits (Social Security & Workers' Compensation) are usually provided by the employer.

- Part-time jobs usually offer less job security.

Many part-time positions are long-term. Some are designed by employers to attract and keep workers who have specific skills the organization needs.

Some service firms (retail stores, restaurants, banks, etc.) operate profitably only because a vast majority of their personnel are part-timers.

Some workers are used only during "peak" periods when the business is serving more customers. Thus part-time employees give many types of organizations flexibility and lower labor costs.

IS A TEMP A PART-TIMER?

Whether a temp is a part-timer is often a matter of opinion. In general, however, there are five ways to distinguish a temp from a typical part-timer:

▶ A temp normally works through an agency. The agency recruits, interviews and hires workers and then places them with organizations *at a profit*.

▶ In most cases, the agency takes care of Social Security, Workers' Compensation, and may provide additional benefits.

▶ The employing organization pays the temp agency, which in turn pays the employee.

▶ Temps often work full-time for short periods in one organization and then, through the help of the agency, move on to a new firm.

▶ When a temp employee's work is unsatisfactory, the employer contacts the agency, which is responsible for the performance of the worker.

Organizations hire temps when they have an immediate but temporary need for one or more full-timers with specific skills.

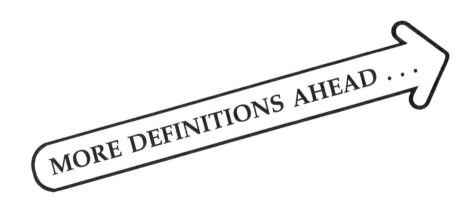

MORE DEFINITIONS AHEAD . . .

CONTRACT EMPLOYEES, FREE-LANCERS, AND CONSULTANTS

Some employees prefer to *contract* out their services rather than be on a regular payroll. Like entrepreneurs, they wish to stay independent. To do this, they make their own Social Security payments and pay for any other benefits they deem necessary.

For example, a lawyer agrees to be on the staff of a law firm but desires to be independent and, when the opportunity surfaces, offer her services to outside clients. Instead of being on a payroll, the lawyer negotiates an annual contract with the firm and takes care of her own benefits.

Gardeners are, in effect, contract employees. They offer to landscape a home under a verbal contract for a set amount each month. Sometimes high-level executives sign written contracts with corporations to provide their services for two or three years at a time. The same is true of coaches in professional sports.

What are the advantages? To many, it provides opportunities to negotiate their services and maintain greater flexibility and more independence. In some cases, there are tax advantages.

Many similarities exist between contract employees and *free-lancers*. Free-lancers, however, usually work in or out of their homes and may serve many different clients at the same times. Artists, for instance, usually offer their services free-lance by spreading themselves around among a variety of clients. Contract employees usually tie themselves down on a part- or full-time basis to one or two clients.

Consultants are experts in special areas and are usually brought into organizations on a short-term basis to help solve recognized problems. Consultants sometimes work out of their homes and serve a number of firms concurrently. Many highly trained specialists continue to work part-time as consultants after retirement.

The term "contingent worker" is frequently used to signify any individual who does not work a full forty-hour week with comprehensive benefits. Part-timers, temps, free-lancers, contract employees and consultants all fall under this "contingency" umbrella.

PART-TIMERS: FROM EXTRANEOUS TO ESSENTIAL

There was a time when part-timers were viewed primarily as helpers who came aboard to do menial tasks. Often they were considered second-class employees. As long as they got their jobs done, supervisors and full-timers pretty much ignored them.

Not so, today! Three significant changes in attitude have taken place that have given part-timers higher, if not equal, status.

1. Part-timers today are employed at all levels. Many do highly skilled work. Some are managers or supervisors. A few are treated more like consultants than part-timers.

2. Part-timers once were kept in one classification while full-timers were in another. Today we recognize that both full- and part-timers can and should be on the same team. In certain work environments, we know that some part-timers can produce as much or more than full-timers. In other words, it is not how many hours you work but how much you produce that is important. Flexible scheduling has assisted the change in this attitude.

3. As we have moved from a manufacturing to a service economy, retailers, restaurants, offices, airlines, etc., have recognized that part-timers are, in effect, prime-timers. In other words, they work when they are needed most. An enthusiastic prime-timer (working twenty-five hours per week when customer traffic is heavy) can often contribute as much as a full-timer. Here again, the value of part-timers is being measured more and more on services contributed, not time spent.

These and other attitudinal changes toward part-timers are raising their status, pay and benefits.

THE CORE-RING APPROACH

To determine the best mix of full-time versus contingent workers, human resource managers are turning to the core-ring approach. As illustrated below, *core* employees constitute the full-time, regular workforce. They are the heart of the organization and, as such, receive comprehensive benefits of many kinds.

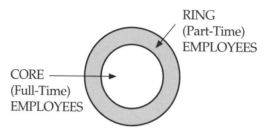

Contingent workers, on the other hand, make up the outer *ring* of employees. This part of the workforce is made up of part-timers, temps, free-lancers and consultants. Although some permanent part-timers may have as much job security as do full-timers, most do not. Typically, they do not earn pensions, participate in profit-sharing plans, or receive paid vacations. Often they are used to fine-tune payrolls to match business cycles. It is estimated that there are about 30 million contingent workers. More than 20 million are part-timers. On the average, for every $1.00 received in pay and benefits by core workers, those in the outer ring receive about $.63. Eventually, it is predicted, one out of three employees will be ring workers.

The following illustration shows the ways some types of organizations have learned how to compete effectively by using more contingent workers than core employees.

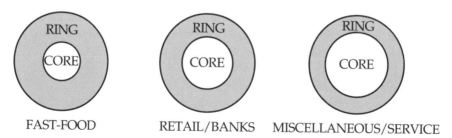

Each firm *must* design its own special mix. Core-rings come in all possible varieties. For example, some firms employ many part-timers for many different work schedules, paying minimum wages and minimal benefits. On the other end of the spectrum is a firm that employs part-timers at different hours, pays substantially above minimum wage, offers greater benefits, and offers incentives to those who stay longer. Although federal legislation to set standards for part-timers is under consideration, little control is exercised at this point.

EMPLOYER ATTITUDES TOWARD PART-TIMERS

To gain some insights into current attitudes of employers toward part-timers, the author informally interviewed a random mix of more than forty owners and managers in a variety of organizations. Responses revealed the following:

- Most said that on an hour-by-hour basis, they could easily identify one or more part-timers who out-performed the average full-timer.

- Only three employers would prefer to work exclusively with full-timers.

- Seven preferred to work with part-timers over others because their energy and enthusiasm was contagious.

- Most admitted that forming effective work teams with both full and part-time employees was more difficult.

- It became obvious that some employers gained measurably greater commitment from part-timers than did others.

- Thirty percent of those from large organizations stated that their firms offered full-time positions (and increased benefits) to part-timers after one year of service.

- Some owners and managers took personal pride in being identified as individuals who work well with part-timers.

- Only a few people indicated that one group (regular or part-timers) presented them with more problems than the other.

- College students and more experienced adults were chosen equally as part-timers.

MOVING FROM FULL- TO PART-TIMERS

Now that almost all organizations are taking a second and third look at their labor costs, part-timers are becoming increasingly popular. Moving from full-timers to part-timers is not, however, an easy decision. Many factors are involved, including:

- How much might labor costs be reduced?

- Would higher productivity cause quality to drop?

- What would be the long-term impact on the profits of a high turnover rate?

- Can part-timers have a positive influence on the productivity of full-timers?

- Does it take a new attitude among full-timers and supervisors to gain high productivity from part-timers?

The next section will explore these and other questions. If you own a small business, you will need to think deeply about the kind of business you operate. If you are an executive with a large firm, you will need to analyze the possible use of more part-timers on a department-by-department basis. If you are a first-line supervisor, you may now need to view the use of part-timers differently than in the past.

Not all organizations are structured to make the best use of part-timers, but most can profit from using them more than they have in the past.

CAN LABOR COSTS BE LOWERED?

As domestic and international competition becomes more aggressive, organizations have been restructuring and downsizing themselves so they can survive. As this competition involves all segments of our economy, it is only natural that many managers are looking to see if labor costs can be reduced through the use of more part-timers.

There are two reasons why part-timers are usually less expensive to have on a payroll.

1. **Part-timers often, but not always, fall on the lower end of the pay scale.** Much of this results from the fact that most part-timers start with beginning or entry-level jobs. There are, however, exceptions. Sometimes a highly skilled professional insists on part-time employment either to join or stay with an organization. Such individuals want to pursue other interests.

2. **Part-timers normally receive fewer company-paid benefits.** Many full-timers in higher wage brackets receive more comprehensive benefits—benefits which can equal as much as 40 percent of their regular pay. Part-timers, on the other hand, may receive only the basic benefits (Social Security and Workers' Compensation). Other benefits (medical) may be available at good rates should employees wish to pay for them.

> The following figures illustrate the possible savings involved:
>
> | *FULL-TIME* | *PART-TIME* |
> |---|---|
> | $12.00 per hour pay | $ 8.00 per hour pay |
> | 4.00 in benefits | 2.00 in benefits |
> | $16.00 per hour | $10.00 per hour |

The above figures, of course, are for illustration purposes only. In many situations, the difference is far more dramatic. One also must consider that some full-timers may *work* only six or seven out of eight hours on the job because of slow periods, poor work scheduling, etc., whereas part-timers employed for four hours may actually work at top performance for almost the entire period.

CAN LABOR COSTS BE LOWERED?
(continued)

Each small business or large corporation must look at all of the elements involved in estimating cost per hour of full-timers versus part-timers. Here are the primary elements:

Productivity

Part-timers should be integrated into the workplace only when their participation contributes measurably to higher productivity. On one end of the spectrum, fast-food and other retail operations are built around and survive only because of part-time employees. On the other end, nonservice corporations, such as factories, may only be able to use a few part-timers to improve productivity.

Quality

Part-timers should never be used just to fill slots without regard to quality of their performance. Rather, they should be used only when the quality level remains the same or improves over that provided by full-timers. One must recognize, however, that the part-timer may require additional training and supervision.

Stress

Employing part-timers in a few organizations might place additional stress on full-timers or supervisors and, thus, cause their productivity to diminish. More often, however, the enthusiasm of the part-timers (especially those who are younger) may alleviate some job stress, and productivity will increase. In short, managers should ask themselves: "What effect will the addition of more part-timers have on the *total morale* of the organization?

Goals

Reducing labor costs is important—maybe critical—but will the replacement of full-timers with part-timers help an organization reach its long-term goals? Ask yourself, "Will we be stronger in the future if we stay with a larger core of full-timers?" "Will a larger ring of part-timers help or hinder the quality of our workforce down the road?" "Is the employment of more part-timers a temporary expediency leading to future problems?"

THE FAST TURNOVER DISADVANTAGE

The major disadvantage of having part-timers on a payroll is excessive personnel turnover. Although some part-timers keep their three- or four-hour-per-week jobs year after year, most part-timers do not make long-term commitments to their jobs. Their main focus in life is elsewhere—earning a college degree, taking care of children, working with a spouse or holding down a second part-time job they like better.

As a result, an organization can employ, process and train a part-time worker, only to have the individual leave after a few days or a week, or not even show up for work at all. When this happens, the firm loses its investment.

Overcoming the Disadvantages

Organizations that depend upon part-timers to assure profitability learn to live with this disadvantage by being more:

- ✓ *astute* in the employment process

- ✓ *skillful* at keeping part-timers happy and involved

- ✓ *creative* at flexible scheduling and many other techniques

Those that operate with large numbers of part-timers learn to:

- ✓ *accept* the "temporariness" factor

- ✓ *work* to gain maximum productivity from part-time employees during the period of their employment

- ✓ *learn* to tolerate the additional mistakes many part-timers make

- ✓ *avoid* assigning them projects that have long training cycles or follow-through periods

THE THREE E'S: ENERGY, ENTHUSIASM AND EXCITEMENT

Surveys indicate that when younger workers are treated in a sensitive manner, they often contribute more energy, enthusiasm and excitement—the "Three E's"—to the work environment than do full-timers. Psychologists have recognized for years that the traditional eight-hour work day can degrade productivity. Just the thought of having to work a full day, for days and weeks in a row, whether there is enough work to do or not, can drag a person down.

Many seasoned full-timers admit that they like working with inexperienced people because some of their energy, enthusiasm and excitement brushes off on them. How does this happen? How can the right mix of part-timers and full-timers bring more of the following E's into the workplace?

Energy Part-timers may or may not arrive with more energy, but they have more to devote to the hours they do work. Part-timers often *need* to work more to get away from home responsibilities or school studies, or to have some social contact with others. With fewer hours to work, less job fatigue occurs.

Enthusiasm Although part-timers generally make less money, the income often means more to them. This is especially true of "first job" part-timers. Moreover, the distance from home duties or academic work has a way of *releasing* enthusiasm. Full-timers may have the capacity for enthusiasm, but it stays bottled-up within them.

Excitement Enthusiasm on the part of a few can breathe more life into others. New-to-the-work force part-timers want to learn how to deal with experienced employees, to learn things that bore full-timers. They bring enthusiasm to learn with them.

Having part-timers can boost the morale and productivity of the full-timers. In short, it can be a profitable mix beyond the lower labor costs. More on this later.

Case Studies: Two Success Stories

Case #1: When her children were all in high school, Genevieve decided to seek a part-time job. A creative college graduate with excellent English-language skills, she was hired on a twenty-hour-per-week basis to assist in a rather small marketing department for a food distributor. It wasn't long before the marketing manager noticed that Genevieve was submitting as many creative ideas as the full-timers, and several of her ideas showed great promise. Later, the manager noticed that the full-timers were more creative, productive and competitive than they had been before Genevieve joined the department.

Case #2: Palmer was finishing up his senior year as a journalism major when he landed a part-time job on a small weekly newspaper. Palmer's assignment was to write stories of secondary interest that full-timers had no time to cover. Soon some of the secondary events Palmer covered became primary stories because they were well written and often communicated a sense of humor—something badly needed by the newspaper. The editor noticed improvements in many articles submitted and decided to offer Palmer a full-time position before he received his degree.

Two factors need to be present for part-timers to motivate full-timers. The part-timer needs to work close to others doing the same type of work, preferably in a team arrangement or, at least, in the same small department. The immediate supervisor or manager of the part-timer needs to give the individual all possible support and training. Only when the manager can bring out the best in the part-timer can that worker motivate full-timers to increase their productivity.

It may, however, be impossible to get full-timers to admit that this has happened!

CONVERTING TO PART-TIMERS: WHICH FIRMS WILL SUCCEED?

Many factors are involved in deciding which organizations should expand their part-time employee mix. The following priority list offers some useful generalities. See if you agree that these types of firms should hire more part-timers.

▶ Small service firms, especially those just starting out. Think of independent restaurants, retail stores and similar organizations that are open odd hours or have peak periods of activity.

▶ Small product-manufacturing or -development firms that have not yet been able to determine the size of their market. Such organizations can use part-time and "on call" employees to develop their full-time positions.

▶ Larger service-oriented firms that are in a growth pattern and need part-timers to help during "peak" periods.

▶ Larger product-oriented firms that are growing and that need part-timers to do short shifts (four hours instead of eight?) to meet demand without increasing overhead costs too fast.

▶ Service firms that are trying to survive—that is, that need to cut costs through the use of more part-timers without endangering the productivity (and evoking the wrath) of full-timers. Such a move has a lower priority because of the higher risks. In some instances, the firm might have waited too long to shift from full- to part-timers.

Each organization has different factors to deal with and, only through careful evaluation, can the best decision be made. In some organizations the transition can be made within one or two years; in others it might take five or ten years. A few should probably stay with a simple full-time workforce.

CHECK YOUR ATTITUDE

Self-Test: What Is Your Attitude Toward Part-Timers?

This exercise will assist you in assessing your present attitude toward the performance of part-time versus full-time employees. Listed in the middle of the page are work factors employers frequently use to appraise employees. Rate how you believe full-time employees compare to part-time employees in each category.

EXPECTED BEHAVIOR

Full-Time Employees		Work Factors	Part-Time Employees	
Excellent	Poor		Excellent	Poor
☐	☐	Responsibility	☐	☐
☐	☐	Absenteeism	☐	☐
☐	☐	Quality of Work	☐	☐
☐	☐	Quantity of Work	☐	☐
☐	☐	Commitment	☐	☐
☐	☐	Concentration	☐	☐
☐	☐	Acceptance of Authority	☐	☐
☐	☐	Cooperation	☐	☐
☐	☐	Follow-through	☐	☐
☐	☐	Initiative	☐	☐
☐	☐	Listening	☐	☐
☐	☐	Self-discipline	☐	☐
☐	☐	Punctuality	☐	☐
☐	☐	Satisfying Customers	☐	☐
☐	☐	Violating Rules	☐	☐
☐	☐	Honesty	☐	☐
☐	☐	Attitude	☐	☐
☐	☐	Consistancy	☐	☐
☐	☐	Willingness to Learn	☐	☐
☐	☐	Creativity	☐	☐
☐	☐	Enthusiasm	☐	☐

TOTAL EXCELLENT RATINGS ☐   **TOTAL EXCELLENT RATINGS** ☐

See page 83 in the back of the book for an interpretation of your ratings.

PART

II

Expanding Your
Labor Pool

RECRUITING PART-TIME EMPLOYEES

If an applicant had the choice of working at Disneyland or a warehouse (same pay and benefits), he or she would probably select Disneyland. Some organizations clearly have a natural advantage in recruiting part-timers. All organizations, however, must try to build a good image (a warehouse can be a great place to work if one is treated well and learns a lot) so that those seeking work are attracted to apply.

Generally speaking, however, it is best to follow the same recruiting techniques in identical channels for part-timers as you would for full-time workers:

College Placement Bureaus

Some organizations—retail operations, restaurants, etc.—build their work force around part-time college students. When this is the case, members of college-placement bureaus (especially if you are located near a college campus) are ideal people to work with on a friendly, permanent basis. Eventually, those on campus will assist you in both recruiting and screening.

Private Employment Agencies

Many organizations rely upon private agencies for part-time help. Some temp agencies also operate as traditional employment offices and can provide part-timers as other agencies do.

Departments of Human Resources

Some organizations find excellent part-timers through local public and private sector personnel offices. Once the interviewers know the qualifications you seek, they are able to do some preliminary screening before sending applicants your way.

Newspaper Want Ads

Daily and weekly newspapers can bring in a wide range of applicants—sometimes more than you can handle easily. Especially during periods of high unemployment, clearly state the qualifications you seek.

RECRUITING PART-TIME EMPLOYEES (continued)

Window Signs and Word-of-Mouth

Many small retailers prefer a simple window sign so that they can attract qualified customers as employees.

Employee Referrals

Your own part-time employees, especially those who take pride in their performance, are often enthusiastic about inviting their friends to apply. Many employees, both full- and part-time, enjoy being involved in the recruitment process.

Obviously, the better you treat employees, the better the reputation your organization earns in a community. Firms that are sensitive to the needs of their people almost always attract more qualified part-timers when a vacancy occurs.

INTERVIEWING APPLICANTS

In addition to normal interview techniques (adhering to fair employment practices, giving applicants the opportunity to ask questions, and other normal procedures) those who interview part-timers can benefit from the following tips:

- Try to discover if the applicant can achieve a good balance between a part-time job and his or her primary focus. For example, if the applicant is a full-time student, will she or he be able to maintain high grades and high job performance at the same time?

- Determine how responsible and committed is the part-time prospect. Will he or she take a part-time entry-level job seriously and deliver high productivity?

- Find out if the part-time applicant has the special skills the job requires or the aptitude and attitude necessary to pick up such skills quickly.

- Beware of applicants who are simply looking for a fill-in job to make a few dollars for a week or so. Those who last only a few weeks do nothing but increase your processing and training costs without making a corresponding contribution of productivity. The ideal part-timers are those who will give you their best over an extended period of time. In this respect, mature individuals who want only part-time work until children are older offer excellent prospects.

One effective technique is to find models—current employees who perform well in their part-time jobs. Compare job applicants with these models.

FOUR HIRING MISTAKES

1. If there are other equally qualified applicants, avoid hiring someone who is currently dealing with a major personal problem. Although the individual may be qualified, the personal problem may overshadow the job performance. For example, Mr. Webb has all of the skills you seek, but he has confided during the interview that he is going through a difficult divorce and has two teenagers over whom he has lost control. Moreover, his doctor has advised against him working more than twenty hours per week.

2. Never hire anyone without specifying a "trial period" involved. State that this policy is for the benefit of both parties to evaluate each other and that either party can make the final decision on or before the end of the trial period.

3. Avoid tokenism, but consider the need to provide opportunities to minority groups based upon the skills they possess in competition with others for a specific job. Race, cultural backgrounds, age, sex and handicaps should not be issues. To employ someone who is not qualified is not doing the person hired a favor, is not fair to qualified applicants or the existing employees, and eventually will backfire.

4. Try not to overidentify with an applicant to the point you show favoritism. Sometimes interviewers are so taken by a part-time applicant that they allow their bias or a favorable first impression to overinfluence their better judgment. For example, a few months ago Julie, a professional interviewer, hired a foreign student who charmed her into throwing away the rules. Yesterday the store detective discovered the part-timer had established a ring of other employees who were stealing merchandise and selling it in a flea market during off hours.

ORIENTATION AND TRAINING

Here are ten tips to assist small business owners and supervisors achieve the highest possible productivity levels from part-timers. Please prioritize them according to their usefulness for your type of operation.

_____ View all part-timers as interns who want to learn as well as earn. Hold them to the same high standards you would full-timers even though their pay per hour and benefits may be less.

_____ Provide an employee handbook and stress the importance of following the rules. Hand out a policy statement prepared especially for part-timers. (See page 30.)

_____ Assign part-timers a sponsor or mentor to assist them in picking up skills and positive attitudes. Experienced, long-term part-timers can do as well or better as sponsors than some full-timers.

_____ Either through individual counseling or in a classroom, stress and discuss quality standards within your organization.

_____ Emphasize customer-service standards.

_____ Consider the long-term possibilities of converting a part-timer into a full-timer. Provide part-timers who have good records preference for full-time openings.

_____ Encourage part-timers to balance outside responsibilities with work assignments. Many retail operations require part-timers to provide and arrange for their own replacements (from the pool of other part-timers) when absent. Discuss your policy with new part-timers.

_____ Reinforce positive behavior—especially during the first days and weeks. Pay as many compliments as possible.

_____ Consult with a new part-timer at the end of the first week or after twenty hours on the job.

_____ Consult with a new part-timer at the end of the first month.

For a useful book on new employee orientation, order *Your First Thirty Days,* by Elwood N. Chapman, Crisp Publications, Inc., Menlo Park, CA 1990.

TRAINING IMPLICATIONS

You are the director of human resources. You believe your firm can profit by doubling the number of part-timers. This would be accomplished through attrition. How would you go about making such a change in the employee mix?

The following four steps are recommended:

Step 1

Get your staff involved. Present your basic plan to all department members. It is especially important that the individual responsible for training and/or the person in charge of interviewing new employees become committed to the project. To gain this commitment, encourage their input in a series of meetings to perfect your plan. Assign one individual to research the legal aspects of your plan. What are the minimal benefits that must be provided to a part-time employee? Is it legal to abolish a full-time position and replace it with a part-time one? How can you make the change without hurting the morale of full-timers?

Step 2

Win the full support of upper management. This means making a presentation to change the mind-set of senior managers so they will be more willing to fill certain full-time positions with part-timers. Present figures showing how much your project will save in labor costs and state how it is possible to increase productivity as you reach this goal.

Step 3

Prepare all supervisors. Recognize that the primary responsibility for using more part-timers profitably is in the hands of the direct supervisor. She or he must know the skills involved in each job, where changes in the mix should be considered, and when and how such improvements might be made. *Experimentation must take place within departments with the full support of the supervisor or team leader.* As the director of human resources, you should structure a seminar for all supervisors. During such a seminar, the complete program should be presented and input requested. At the finish offer an invitation to any supervisor wishing to set up a model mix in his or her department.

Attitudes do not change quickly when one has operated with only full-timers in a department, so anticipate opposition from some quarters. Stress over and over that greater productivity at lower per-hour cost is the goal.

Stress also that every attempt will be made to ensure that the new policy on part-timers does not threaten full-time employees.

Step 4

Inform all employees on the new policy regarding part-timers for the following reasons: (1) to keep false rumors from spreading; (2) to invite input; (3) to communicate that jobs will be more secure if the new policy succeeds in making the firm more profitable; (4) to invite any present full-timers who wish to switch to part-time in the future to talk to their supervisor; (5) to prepare full-timers to accept and assist any part-timers who will join their departments in the future.

The breadth of the training implications is challenging. Everything from a policy to recruit the best available part-timers to preparing "sponsors" to help those hired to adjust is involved.

Changing the mix of employees in an organization clearly takes time, effort and coordination.

A MESSAGE FOR NEW EMPLOYEES

Orientation Message for
New Part-Time Employees

1. We currently have _____ part-time employees versus _____ full-timers. This is a ratio of _____ to _____.

2. Whenever possible, it is our policy to select members of our full-time staff from our pool of part-timers.

3. If you aspire to a full-time or another part-time position, we encourage you to discuss the matter with your immediate supervisor.

4. As a new part-timer, your trial period will be fifteen working days. You can anticipate an informal conference with your supervisor at the end of this period.

5. We respect you and your contribution in the same way we respect that of full-time employees.

6. Your suggestions for improving the productivity of your department and the quality of our operation are taken seriously. Present your suggestions to your immediate supervisor in writing.

7. In return for your high productivity, we will provide you with all possible learning experiences.

8. Please keep in mind that our customers do not know whether you are a full or part-timer. All they are concerned with is the quality of service they receive.

9. If and when you move on to a different career (perhaps one you are preparing for now), we will be pleased to recognize in writing, upon request, the level of contribution you have made to our organization.

10. We are proud of our organization and the contribution we make to our society. We hope you will share this pride with us.

EMPLOYING YOUNG PART-TIMERS

This section is especially designed for those businesses that employ "first-time" workers between the ages of sixteen and twenty-one years. It provides tips to assist the supervisor in the effective management of these younger workers. (The tips will also be helpful with other employees.) It is estimated that more than 70 percent of all part-timers fall into this classification.

As you read each tip, think about whether or not that suggestion will fit comfortably into your present supervisory style. If the idea seems to fit and you can see that it will help you gain greater productivity from part-timers, circle the tip number.

Tips for Supervisors

Tip #1: Capitalize On the Earn-Learn Idea

Tip #2: Trust Your Part-Time Employees

Tip #3: Give Compliments—They're Free!

Tip #4: Ask Part-Timers to Give Their Best

Tip #5: Recognize Young Part-Timers Are Going Through a Transition Period

Tip #6: Use "Fun" to Reward High Productivity

Tip #7: Communicate Errors Without Causing Embarrassment

Tip #8: Accommodate Special-Purpose Absences

Tip #9: Tie Jobs to Long-Term Career Goals

Tip #10: Treat All Employees the Same

Tip #11: Discover Potential Full-Timers

TIP #1: CAPITALIZE ON THE EARN-LEARN IDEA

Young workers are almost as interested in learning as in earning. They recognize they are just starting out and that getting experience is as important as saving a few dollars for new clothes, a car, or whatever.

Learning will help them:

- Deal with experienced adults.
- Get a better job later.
- Communicate better.

You can capitalize on this desire to learn by patiently teaching part-timers how to perform specific tasks that are new to them. Here are some ways to teach young workers:

1. Explain why learning the task is important. If necessary, be sure the learner is positioned to see how it is done. Do not start until you have his or her full attention.

2. Describe, illustrate and demonstrate one important step at a time. Do not give too much information too fast.

3. Have the learner do the job under your supervision so that you can correct any errors. Repeat the performance until it is being done right and then compliment the learner.

4. Tell the learner where to go for help. Check in a few days to see if the learner has become comfortable with the process.

When you help a first-time employee learn a new task, you build confidence in that individual and enhance your own reputation. Decide now to become an outstanding instructor!

Check One Only

❏ **1.** I will improve my teaching techniques by using the four-step procedure.

❏ **2.** I am satisfied with my teaching techniques. No improvements are necessary.

TIP #2: TRUST YOUR PART-TIME EMPLOYEES

Most young part-timers are ready for more responsibility than their parents or teachers have given them so far. It is only natural for parents—and even some teachers—to keep thinking that their children are not as mature as they really are. But you, as a supervisor, see a person who, once given a difficult responsibility, will probably come through.

Like many prophecies, "I trust you" is often self-fulfilling. Once the young part-timer has proved that you can trust her or him, the next time around you can say, "This is a tough assignment, but you have demonstrated that I can trust you. Go to it." Later on, when you give out a new challenge, using the word trust will not be necessary because a strong relationship already will have been built. Both you and the part-timer will want to maintain it.

Surprisingly, a new part-time employee often desires responsibility but does not ask for it. When it is freely given, however, the response is usually more than satisfactory. Young workers often want the acceptance of experienced adults more than we anticipate. All they need is the opportunity to earn it. When the time is right and the opportunity is appropriate, give it to them.

Fulfilling the responsibility will give them confidence in themselves and status among their working peers!

Check One Only

❏ **1.** I am willing to give part-timers under my supervision more responsibility in the future. The risk is worth taking!

❏ **2.** I prefer to assign responsible tasks in my own, slower, time schedule. Young part-timers need to *grow* into responsibilities, not be *thrown* into them too quickly.

TIP #3: GIVE COMPLIMENTS—THEY'RE FREE!

In schools teachers give out grades—good and bad. At home, parents give out rules and deadlines. At work, too many supervisors continue the process by acting as authority figures—barking out orders and chewing out employees whose behavior does not fit their exacting standards. Nothing seems to change.

BUT IT COULD!

A compliment is a formal act or expression of courtesy, respect, admiration, praise or flattery. Many part-timers, still in school and living at home, are hungry for a few personal compliments. Like a plant that needs proper care to grow, young people often need compliments to help them take that last step into being fully productive workers.

There are three ways to pay a deserved compliment:

1. Do it on a one-on-one basis, in private. For example, if you are pleased with the success a new part-timer has made, call him or her into your private office, pay the compliment and ask if there are any problems.

2. Do it in front of a group of co-workers. When everyone on the employee "team" recognizes that one member has excelled in a specific area, it is rewarding for that individual to be honored by a compliment in front of the group. Of course, it must be done in a sensitive manner, and compliments eventually should be spread around the entire group. Avoid playing favorites.

3. Do it in writing. Often this means more and becomes a keepsake or is retained for use in a resume or in other ways.

Paying compliments does not come naturally to many people. But all supervisors should learn to do it in a sincere and natural manner. Compliments speed growth and increase productivity.

Check One Only

❑ **1.** I understand why part-timers need more compliments. I intend to change my behavior and, when deserved, use all three forms in the future.

❑ **2.** I intend to continue my present pattern of paying compliments, because any changes would not fit into my comfort zone.

TIP #4: ASK PART-TIMERS TO GIVE THEIR BEST

"GIVE ME YOUR BEST WHILE YOU ARE HERE."

Admittedly, most part-timers do not have a big stake in the organizations they join.

How can you handle this?

First, *anticipate an early departure.* Recognize that the job they have with you is a fill-in situation. They want the job, they need the job, and they can produce at a high level, but they have laid plans for something else. You are likely to lose them and often relatively soon.

Second, communicate the message that you are happy to have them on board. Then, clearly and with emphasis, say, "While you are here, I will give you as much experience as possible to help you reach your long-range goals. I only ask one thing: *Give me your best while you are here.*

Of course, you may wish to make other comments similar to these:

- "Use this job as a laboratory to improve your communications and human-relations skills."

- "There are many things you can learn from this part-time job that you can take with you into full-time jobs."

- "Use this job to prepare yourself for something better."

You will always know whether or not you have treated your part-time employees in the best possible way by the number who keep in touch with you after they have reached their goals.

Check One Only

❑ **1.** I agree that the best way to achieve high productivity from part-timers is to recognize they may have bigger goals and to ask only that they do their best before they leave.

❑ **2.** I believe that recognizing up front that part-timers will eventually leave only speeds their departure date.

TIP #5: RECOGNIZE YOUNG PART-TIMERS ARE GOING THROUGH A TRANSITION PERIOD

The passage from teenager to young adult is not easy. Those who tackle their first part-time job usually want to be treated as full-fledged adults, but they soon realize that it will take months, perhaps years, for them to fully qualify. As a result, they often live in two worlds.

The Theory X of management accepts the premise that if you give employees too much freedom, they will produce at a low level and probably get into trouble. Thus Theory X supervisors believe in strong discipline, close supervision and little or no nonwork-related activity. A Theory X supervisor is 98 percent business.

The Theory Y of management states that you can get greater productivity out of people by giving them more freedom under which to operate. Theory Y managers believe in group involvement, employee empowerment and operating as a "team." Normally they exert less authority and provide more involvement.

With young part-timers the best approach is a combination: Have a few clear and fast rules (strong discipline) but allow some room for them to express themselves, enjoy parts of their work, and *grow into adult behavior.* In short, recognize that some juvenile behavior will occur.

Here are three suggestions:

1. When young part-timers make mistakes, do not come down hard on them. They know they have done something wrong and that you and their peers know it.

2. Do your best to inform, teach and work with your full-time employees so that they, too, will understand the young part-timer. Most full-time co-workers do an excellent job with part-timers when given the responsibility to act as a sponsor or mentor.

3. Recognize that expecting young part-timers consistently to act as an adult on the job may be unrealistic. They may need more coaching and counseling than others to maintain high-productivity standards.

Compassion backed by a few firm rules will help create the most productive work environment.

Check One Only

❏ **1.** I would lean in the direction of Theory X.

❏ **2.** I would lean in the direction of Theory Y.

TIP #6: USE "FUN" TO REWARD HIGH PRODUCTIVITY

I once met the owner of a fast-food franchise who knew how to work with young part-timers. One of his techniques was to authorize an "ice fight" at the close of business each Saturday night. After the last customer had departed, he would permit those who wanted to participate to throw ice the consistency of snow at each other, clean up the mess and then have "post-party" refreshments. When asked what he accomplished in permitting this, he replied: "Young people work hard for me, and now and then they need to let off steam. A good snow fight allows them to release their frustrations. It also seems to help them form into more of a team."

As you weave a little fun into your own operation, keep the following in mind:

▶ *Young workers will, at times, overdo it.* It is sometimes difficult for them to know when to stop. After all, they are *growing into* the world of work and they need time to make a full transition. That is why you must set firm rules and stick with them.

▶ With just a little training, young part-timers can be excellent with customers. They must be taught, however, that the customer deserves immediate attention and that they must be formal in their approach. It is possible to enjoy customers, but becoming too personal too soon can be offensive. Many young people need a little help in developing just the right "touch."

Check One Only

❑ **1.** Under certain circumstances and depending upon how many part-timers are present, I am willing to set aside some "fun time" as a reward to high productivity.

❑ **2.** I would hesitate to set aside "fun time" as a reward for part-time or any workers. Work is work.

TIP #7: COMMUNICATE ERRORS WITHOUT CAUSING EMBARRASSMENT

Many young workers embarrass easily. Some of this is because they are sensitive to peer pressure. Some stems from the fact that they have yet to build strong self-images. Therefore, supervise young part-timers with kid gloves.

Here are some suggestions that will assist you in getting higher productivity from part-timers instead of dissipating their enthusiasm through embarrassment:

▶ Accept mistakes quietly. If an employee makes a noticeable and unnecessary mistake, work with him or her to avoid future errors, but do it in a way that would not be embarrassing.

▶ Try to avoid formal counseling behind closed doors. You may be able to solve problems through stand-up counseling in a casual manner, as long as you are out of earshot of others.

▶ Where possible, laugh off slight mistakes made in front of peers.

▶ If you discover someone doing a task the wrong way, make the correction by demonstrating the better way and moving on. Don't make a big thing of it.

▶ When correcting part-timers, try to pay them a sincere compliment on some other area of their work.

▶ Do not hesitate to step in to keep employees from embarrassing each other. Train others to be sensitive in the way they work with less-experienced workers.

▶ In assigning part-timers to new jobs, provide a full- or part-time sponsor to show them the way and keep them from embarrassment.

▶ Do whatever it takes to help part-timers who work for you to build a stronger self-image. Let them know you are behind them all the way.

Check One Only

❑ **1.** I believe that supervisors who protect their part-time employees from embarrassment receive higher productivity from all employees.

❑ **2.** I believe that it is a mistake to protect young part-timers from embarrassing situations. They grow more when they face and correct difficult situations on their own.

TIP #8: ACCOMMODATE SPECIAL-PURPOSE ABSENCES

Absenteeism is always a serious, costly problem. Do not tolerate chronic absenteeism of part-timers. Young part-timers, however, may have special events in their lives—school events such as important ball games, special parties such as a senior prom, and family events where they are pressured by parents to be present. Here, accommodation on your part would be smart. It is likely that the part-timer will appreciate your understanding so much that he or she will produce more for you in the long run.

Here are some tips to minimize the problem:

1. If you have enough part-timers, institute a policy where the absent worker is responsible for finding his or her replacement among those on your payroll.

2. Always require advance notice if you, the supervisor, must find the replacement.

3. Give special considerations only to those who are consistently on time.

4. Treat all part-timers equally.

5. Compliment those who maintain the best attendance records.

6. When a part-timer becomes ill at the last moment, have a responsible person call you, the supervisor, so that you can arrange a replacement.

Check One Only

❑ 1. I am in favor of going all-out to accommodate part-timers who have special events connected with school or family.

❑ 2. The rules that apply to other employees should apply equally to part-timers. Special consideration should not be provided.

TIP #9: TIE JOBS TO LONG-TERM CAREER GOALS

Although part-timers' specific tasks may not relate directly to a future career, it is a good idea to discover what part-timers' career goals may be. When possible, point out that what they learn might help them in the future.

Here are some fundamentals that a part-timer can learn from almost *any* job:

▶ *Dealing with adults:* Most young part-timers need to learn to work with adults as equals. You are performing a great service if you help them do this. Your role as supervisor or owner is significant to them. If they get along well with you, they have taken a big step forward.

▶ *Self-discipline:* A job requires a different kind of self-discipline than is required at school or at home. The conditions are often more hectic and demanding.

▶ *Becoming an effective work team member:* Being part of a work team means considering the safety and productivity of all workers. Playing on a sports team is helpful, but a work team has different rules and demands.

▶ *Developing learning attitudes in a work environment:* No matter how much formal education one receives, starting out in *any* organization requires a learning attitude. The more practice one gets in a part-time job, the better.

As an employer of young part-timers, you can encourage them to reach their long-term career goals—even though it may mean they will leave you sooner. This attitude on your part, however, will encourage them to give you their highest level of productivity while they are with you.

Check One Only

❑ **1.** Pointing out any connections between what a part-timer learns and a future career goal is a good idea.

❑ **2.** Helping students sense such connections is a waste of time.

TIP #10: TREAT ALL EMPLOYEES THE SAME

It is easy to fall into the trap of thinking that part-time employees are second-class, disposable employees whom you keep around to do routine tasks and save money. When you hear expressions such as these, you know that this attitude exists in your organization:

- "He's just here on a part-time basis."

- "Why worry? Those part-timers won't be around long anyway."

Such attitudes can cost an organization. Customers do not know or care whether an employee is full- or part-time; their concern is that they are treated courteously.

- Treat part-timers similarly to full-timers.

- Accept them as full-fledged members of the work team.

- Make them feel that what they do is as important as what full-timers do.

How can you accomplish this?

First, do not keep part-timers in the dark about what is going on. Without full communication, they will feel that they are less important than others—and *their productivity will show it!*

Second, give part-timers credit when due. When they do good work, sometimes superior to what full-timers do, they deserve praise.

Third, invite them to company functions. If part-timers are to feel they are a real part of an organization, they need to be involved in company events. They need not be paid at higher levels, and they need not receive full benefits, but they need to feel they *belong.*

Check One Only

❑ **1.** I agree that part-timers should receive first-class treatment.

❑ **2.** Part-timers are adjuncts to the full-time workforce. As such, they need not receive the same treatment as those who work full-time and devote much of their lives to the organization.

TIP #11: DISCOVER POTENTIAL FULL-TIMERS

Every time you employ a part-timer, you may want to consider her or his potential as a permanent member of your staff. Part-timers often constitute a pool of possible full-timers. The full-time jobs with comprehensive benefits should be available only to those who have proved themselves as part-timers. As traditional forty-hour positions become scarcer and more valuable, many who accept part-time jobs will have their eyes on full-time positions from the very start. Vying for such jobs will provide healthy competition and increase productivity among part-timers. This is likely to become the pattern of the future.

Here are three suggestions on how to treat part-timers who seek full-time positions in your organization:

1. Give these individuals special assignments to test their skills, but do not give them special treatment. It is okay to give more responsibility to potential full-timers, but they should not be granted special privileges.

2. Counsel all employees equally, but give part-timers who wish to become full-timers advice that will help them reach their long-term goals with you.

3. Do not make unrealistic promises. Rather, let part-timers make their decisions based upon both positive and negative factors at your organization. Avoid oversell at all costs!

Check One Only

❏ 1. Discovering and converting part-timers into long-term employees is a major advantage to having part-timers in the first place.

❏ 2. I would not make any special effort to convert part-timers into full-timers.

TIP #12: REVIEW, PRIORITIZE AND SUBMIT A TIP OF YOUR OWN

Please review the eleven tips presented and prioritize them in the spaces provided below. List what you feel to be the most important tip in line number 1, your second most important tip in line 2, and so on, until you have listed all eleven suggestions.

1. _____
2. _____
3. _____
4. _____
5. _____
6. _____
7. _____
8. _____
9. _____
10. _____
11. _____

Wind up this part of the book by writing in the space below a tip of your own—one that will enable supervisors to gain more productivity from part-time workers.

_____

_____

_____

_____

_____

_____

_____

_____

Quiz: Understanding Younger Part-Timers

Measure the progress you are making by taking this quiz. Place a checkmark under "True" if you believe the answer to be true; place a checkmark under "False" if you think it is false. Correct answers will be found on page 83 at the back of the book.

TRUE   **FALSE**

_____   _____   1. Learning is more important to young part-timers than the money they earn.

_____   _____   2. The big problem with young part-timers is that they are not ready to assume responsibilities.

_____   _____   3. Supervisors of young part-timers should set themselves up as authority figures.

_____   _____   4. It is not how long employees stay with an organization, but what they produce as they pass through.

_____   _____   5. The Theory Y management style is to facilitate group involvement without imposing strong discipline.

_____   _____   6. Permitting young part-timers to have a little fun where they work encourages a breakdown in authority.

_____   _____   7. Peer pressure and weak self-images make it difficult to embarrass young workers.

_____   _____   8. Allowing young part-timers to be absent for special occasions, such as those connected with school activities, is a mistake.

_____   _____   9. Young workers can learn certain human principles that will assist them no matter what their careers may be.

_____   _____   10. Supervised by a sensitive, understanding person, part-timers can produce more per hour than full-timers.

TOTAL CORRECT [   ]

THE RETIREE LABOR MARKET

Today more retirees want jobs—to supplement their incomes, give themselves social contacts and challenge themselves. Why is this true?

- People tend to retire at an earlier age.

- Retirees live longer, are more agile and have greater endurance.

- Most retirees remain mentally alert.

- Most retirees recognize that they need a challenge beyond pure leisure to keep themselves involved and happy.

Hits and Myths

HITS	MYTHS
These advantages of hiring older part-timers are hits:	*These so-called disadvantages are myths:*
▶ Many retired part-timers offer skills and talents that your organization cannot find elsewhere.	▶ *Older workers are too slow physically.* This is not the case—it's the exception, not the rule.
▶ Retirees are the most dependable and reliable part-timers in the labor market today.	▶ *Older workers want to take over.* Most retirees recognize that as part-timers they neither qualify for, nor desire, a management position.
▶ Most older workers know how to blend in with younger workers, and thus can contribute to higher productivity both through their own work and through helping others produce more.	▶ *Older people can't adjust.* There is no evidence that retirees who re-enter the labor market are slow to adjust to new demands.
▶ Part-time retirees are especially effective on projects where they can demonstrate their reliability and follow-through.	▶ *Older people just create problems.* Most work in harmony with co-workers and managerment. They appreciate the opportunity to solve problems, not create them.

GET HIGHER PRODUCTIVITY FROM PART-TIME RETIREES

Just as young part-timers respond better to certain kinds of supervision, so do retirees. Listed below are ten ways to increase the productivity of older workers and encourage them to stay around longer and contribute more to your organization:

1. Retired workers do not seek special favors, but they feel their years of experience have earned them dignity and respect.

2. Retirees like to think that they are in the mainstream with younger workers and can handle problems others face. When a supervisor makes an older employee feel he or she is up-to-date and "with it," greater productivity ensues.

3. Mature people work for appreciation as well as for money.

4. Older workers like to be given special assignments or small projects so they can demonstrate their skills and follow-through.

5. Retirees often provide sensitive leadership without being designated as leaders.

6. Retired workers usually make excellent sponsors for younger part-timers. They enjoy teaching what they have learned.

7. Older workers can usually accept criticism and make adjustments as well as others. A supervisor should not hold back on giving such criticism as long as it is done in private. Again, most retirees do not want special favors.

8. Asking senior part-timers what specific tasks they would prefer is often a good idea. They frequently select low-prestige jobs to demonstrate their willingness to contribute from any position.

9. It is okay to ask capable part-time retirees to submit in private any suggestions to improve productivity. Their insights are often valuable.

10. Part-time retirees want to be accepted as members of the "team" and do their part or more. Except for special projects, they do not want to be isolated.

SCREENING RETIREES OLDER THAN SIXTY-FIVE

When screening retirees for employment, follow all standard procedures. Also consider the following issues. Implementing these suggestions will make more retirees successful in holding down part-time jobs and will open the market wider for retirees in the future.

▶ **Know that health considerations are a mutual concern.**   Point out to the applicant that most health or disability problems can probably be handled, but discuss them openly from the start.

▶ **Consider transportation problems in advance.**   Some retirees do not have automobiles, so it is important to find part-time retirees who live close to where they will work or who have access to public transportation. Transportation can be more of a problem with older workers.

▶ **Adjust hours to Social Security payments.**   If retirees are already drawing Social Security payments, you may have to restrict the hours worked so that their income falls within the limitations. When earnings pass over a certain limit, one dollar must be payed back through taxes for each two dollars earned.

▶ **Mesh current skills to tasks.**   With perhaps forty years of work experience behind her or him, a retiree (with a little brushing up) may have a plethora of skills. You must discover if any skills fit the tasks to be performed in available jobs. Do all of this before making an employment commitment.

▶ **Beware of inflexibility.**   It is always difficult and often impossible to weave overqualified, rigid individuals into a department. In most cases, it is probably best to hire another equally qualified applicant, unless you have a special project or task to be performed where flexibility is not as important.

▶ **Watch for retirees who talk too much.** It may be best to pass on an applicant who appears to have the need to talk excessively. Many seniors are lonely, and they may want a job just to have people to talk to. Social conversations and getting work out are two different things.

If you discover that the applicant has worked part-time for another employer since retirement, call for a reference.

To protect yourself, make sure that both you and the retiree clearly understand that the trial period in effect for all employees applies to the retiree as well.

OFFER SPECIAL ORIENTATION COUNSELING

Although retirees should go through the same orientation program designed for all employees, discussing some matters privately with a new older worker would be profitable. Here are some questions you might ask that would give the individual a better chance of making a harmonious and productive adjustment.

1. "One of your challenges will be to get those young enough to be your grandchildren to like and respect you. How would you go about doing this?"

2. "I would like for you to prove that my company is right in its policy to employ retirees. If you can do this, you will be doing other people your age a favor. If this is your wish, how are you going to accomplish such a goal?"

3. "Your supervisor will welcome a few suggestions from you after you have gotten your feet on the ground, but you do not want to 'bug' him or her. When and how do you intend to make suggestions?"

4. "If this job works out, and I believe it will, how will it contribute to a better retirement for you?"

5. "It will be difficult for you not to criticize a few young workers. How do you intend to keep from doing this?"

6. "What do you think your most difficult problem might be?"

7. "What can I do personally to assist you in your adjustment?"

8. "As you know, we have a regular thirty-day trial period. We don't anticipate any problems that will keep you from becoming a long-term part-time employee. But if something you do not anticipate now causes you to reconsider staying with us, will you do me the favor of talking to me in advance?"

The more you can get the retiree to recognize that most retirees do have some adjustment problems, the easier it will be for her or him. The purpose of this interview is to help the person feel comfortable with her or his role. If, through your open discussion, you can discover the main reason the retiree wants to work, you can suggest how he or she can satisfy this need.

On top of everything else, make the meeting nonthreatening and enjoyable for both parties. Make sure the individuals know that you respect them for wanting to come back into the labor market and that you want to make their experience rich and rewarding.

Case Study: Jerry

Jerry is sixty-nine, retired and talented. He started out as a person who enjoyed "tinkering" with machines of all kinds. At one time he owned his own shop. Later, he worked as a machine designer for a larger machine shop. Through all of his working years Jerry maintained what he called his little "invention shop" at home.

Mr. Barr heard about Jerry from a friend and called upon him to see if Jerry qualified as someone who could help him figure out new machines for some of his off-beat clients. When Mr. Barr looked over the "invention shop," he knew he had found the right person.

Would Jerry be interested in a part-time job? Could he turn his retirement hobby into a good-paying job? Would he like to work at home and still be part of a "team" at Mr. Barr's machine-development corporation? Would Jerry like to keep up with new equipment, share ideas with younger minds and know that he is making a contribution? Could a working relationship be customized so that both parties could benefit?

Please assume that through negotiation, a working relationship is established. Who stands to benefit the most? Write your answer and compare it with that of the author on page 84.

_____

_____

_____

_____

Quiz: Understanding Older Part-Timers

Now that you have been introduced to the possibilities connected with employing retirees, are you ready to interview and hear them? To find out, please take this short quiz. Correct answers are on page 84 at the back of the book.

TRUE   **FALSE**

_____   _____   1. Seniors create more problems than younger part-timers.

_____   _____   2. Retirees are more dependable than younger workers.

_____   _____   3. The retiree employment market is expanding.

_____   _____   4. Retirees do not need to be appreciated as much as younger employees.

_____   _____   5. Retirees who work part-time are usually excellent on special projects.

_____   _____   6. It is a good idea to have a two-way counseling session with a retiree just hired.

_____   _____   7. Retirees who are overqualified and inflexible make the best employees.

_____   _____   8. Retirees should be given special privileges because of their age.

_____   _____   9. It is a good idea to pass on an applicant who wants (or needs) to talk excessively.

_____   _____   10. Many employers do not hire qualified seniors because they are afraid the retirees will create problems.

TOTAL CORRECT [   ]

CUSTOMIZING JOBS FOR EXPERIENCED PART-TIMERS

Although young, inexperienced applicants are still most apt to apply for part-time roles, a growing number of experienced workers are seeking employment that will fit into their lifestyles. These persons range from someone who wants to spend time at home with children, to an adult returning for further education, to an unemployed worker willing to accept a part-time position.

What differences will a manager notice between these older experienced part-timers and younger part-timers? Here are some considerations:

▶ Experienced part-timers do not always mix well with younger ones. A primary reason for this is that they have different outside or social interests. A young part-timer may be talking about school and dates while someone older might be concerned with family problems, children and budgets. Obviously, it is easier to build a working team with all young or all experienced workers. Capable supervisors, however, can get solid performance from a mix of both.

▶ Many mature part-timers have less flexible schedules. They may want to leave, for example, when three o'clock arrives so they can pick up their children at school.

▶ Mature part-timers are more apt to be underemployed; thus it may be best to give them more responsible work assignments. When performance is high, early pay adjustments may be in order.

These differences show why minor job customization is in order for those with more experience. This helps integrate the seasoned part-timer into the core work force. When hiring an experienced worker into a part-time role, the primary concern should be assigning the proper type of work. Is there a special job at which this person can contribute more?

If no such jobs are available, then the experienced worker should start in a job identical to that of the inexperienced person and become part of the team without expecting special consideration.

WHAT IS JOB CUSTOMIZATION?

Because more experienced part-timers have already made the transition from inexperienced to seasoned workers, their behavior will be more like that of the mature, full-time worker. Thus, when you fill a part-time job where experience is required, you may need to make special concessions to the prospective part-timer who has the required skills. These adjustments are called customization.

Customization is a good idea when people with high-level skills only want to work part-time. Such an individual has the skills to get a full-time job, but because of other interests (raising children, developing other talents or furthering their education) they opt to work on a part-time basis.

In such cases, customization of jobs may be the answer for both the employer and employee. This section explores the possibilities from both sides.

*Employers'
Needs*

*Seasoned
Workers'
Needs*

Maturity
Experience
Special Talents
High-Level Skills

Adjustments
Job Assignment
Flexible Scheduling
Special Concessions

TYPES OF JOB CUSTOMIZATION

When an employer has a valuable full-time worker who has special skills the organization needs, and the employee decides he or she wants to work less than full-time, the employer might *customize* a part-time job to save the talent. For example:

> *Harold, a computer specialist, decided to return to college for a degree in another discipline. In order to keep Harold's expertise, the firm customized a part-time job to conform to his classroom and study schedule.*

When an employer discovers a mature, highly capable employee in the marketplace who seeks only a part-time job during certain hours, in order to use this talent, the employer might customize a job to entice that worker. For example:

> *Helen, a graphics specialist with excellent writing skills, seeks a part-time role with flexible hours so that she can be the kind of parent she wants to be. When she finds a midsize company that needs some art talent and wants to publish a lively bulletin each week, she sits down with its managers and they work out an arrangement where both parties can get what they want.*

Customization means creating a job that will meet the specifications of a present or prospective employee and, at the same time, serve the organization. Some negotiating usually takes place.

Factors important to the individual include schedule, available transportation, pay, work environment, benefits and job assignment. The factors important to the organization are level of talent, whether a part-time job can be arranged that will serve the firm's need, how the job can be integrated into the work flow, and the availability of proper training and supervision.

Job customization, both full- and part-time, will probably double before the turn of the century.

WHEN DOES JOB CUSTOMIZATION WORK?

Many factors need to be present before customization is given a fair trial:

▶ The special talent the organization seeks is not available within the firm, and employing a full-timer would be too expensive.

▶ The employee must have a flexible working schedule.

▶ The employee should not have an all-consuming outside interest that precludes his or her full concentration on the job.

▶ The cost to the company must be reasonable.

▶ The employee should be able to work well with others and become an excellent team member.

▶ The arrangement should contribute measurably to the firm's productivity and profit.

▶ Both parties should be able to anticipate a high degree of permanence with the arrangement.

▶ The employee should be considered a part-timer and not a consultant with a contract arrangement or a free-lancer who markets his or her talents to a variety of firms on a fee basis.

Obviously, organizations that value customization to gain talent not otherwise available should use caution as they experiment with the process. Once they have achieved success in one area, they could expand into others and establish a standard process.

To encourage the reader to gain additional insights into the potential of customization, two case studies are presented on the following pages.

Customization Case #1

Jean left her position as a computer programmer more than a year ago to finish her master's degree. Last night, she and her husband talked about her going back into the labor market as a part-timer. Jean admitted that she would like to contribute to their income and to have some work contacts while she's in school. Her husband is totally in favor of the move if Jean can find a position that could use her unusually high computer skills, allow her to work two ten-hour shifts per week not more than ten miles from home, and pay an hourly wage commensurate with her abilities. A benefits package, other than the basics, is unimportant, since her husband's position with a large organization provides full coverage for both of them.

Together they construct the following ad to be placed in the business section of a local newspaper.

```
HIGHLY SKILLED COMPUTER PROGRAMMER SEEKS
PART-TIME INVOLVEMENT AS A TROUBLESHOOTER
UNDER A FLEX SCHEDULE.
```

What are Jean's chances of locating a part-time position that will satisfy her desires? Write your answer below and compare it to that of the author on page 84 at the back of the book.

_____

_____

_____

_____

_____

Case Study: Drake

Drake is a literary agent who specializes in movie and television scripts. He is successful because he has built unusually good relationships with a growing number of made-for-television movie producers. Drake's primary problem is that he spends so much time keeping up his contacts that he has little time left to read and evaluate the many scripts that wind up on his desk.

Two years ago Drake helped Rick, a new writer, get an excellent start when Rick's script was purchased by a movie house. Since that time, however, nothing else of Rick's has been accepted. Believing that Rick will eventually become a winner, Drake wants to help him in any way possible.

Yesterday Rick came to see if Drake could help him get a part-time job during his dry spell. Drake agreed to hire Rick to give a first reading to incoming scripts from other authors under the conditions that Rick:

- Work Tuesdays and Thursdays in Drake's office and, while evaluating scripts, answer incoming telephone calls.

- Continue to work as a bartender three evening shifts per week to maintain most of his income.

- Complete one script of his own every two months.

Would this arrangement be a win-win situation for both parties? Write your answer below and compare it with that of the author on page 84 at the back of the book.

_____

_____

_____

_____

_____

_____

Quiz: Job Customization

To verify your understanding of job customization, please place a checkmark under the appropriate column. Correct answers are found on page 84 at the back of the book.

TRUE   **FALSE**

____   ____   1. The practice of customizing part-time jobs is designed to attract consultants and free-lancers.

____   ____   2. Customization will expand because the process is profitable for firms and allows talented people to work part-time while they pursue other interests.

____   ____   3. It is considered unethical for a full-time employee to discuss the possibilities of customization with a present employer.

____   ____   4. An eighteen-year-old part-timer does not normally have a specific skill or talent to justify customization.

____   ____   5. A retiree with special talents should feel free to discuss customization with a prospective employer.

____   ____   6. If an employer split one full-time job into two parts in order to keep two valuable employees who only want part-time work, this would be customization.

____   ____   7. A small business owner who creates a job for a son to help him through college is engaged in customization.

____   ____   8. Customization does not make sense for full-timers.

____   ____   9. Large organizations seldom can benefit from customization.

____   ____   10. Negotiation is not involved in the customization process.

TOTAL CORRECT [ ]

P A R T

III

Hiring Part-Timers: Management Considerations

CHANGING EMPLOYEE CULTURES

Employing more part-timers presents many challenges. Give top priority to the impact of more part-timers on the full-time workforce. If full-timers not only welcome part-timers but become more productive themselves, then everyone is going to come out ahead. If, however, full-timers resent part-timers and misinterpret their contribution to the firm, the use of more part-timers can be counterproductive.

Compare the differences! Full-timers are steady workers who pick up the pieces when part-timers leave. They assume long-term responsibilities. They are most protective of their roles. Many climb the corporate ladder and make contributions as leaders. On the other hand, some full-timers get into ruts where their productivity falls below the acceptable standard.

Part-timers constitute a mobile culture. They have few ties to their organizations. Sometimes, they disappear before they reach their potential. Many are not interested in full-time roles. But part-timers often bring new ideas, fresh energy and high productivity with them. When this happens, full-timers often benefit the most. For example, part-timers seldom participate in profit-sharing plans although they may contribute to the profit picture. Result? Full-timers pick up some of the profits made possible by part-timers in their profit-sharing plans. In other words, part-timers can make life better for full-timers.

On whom does the brunt fall when a firm converts to using more part-timers?

Initially, it falls on the shoulders of supervisors. Only when supervisors are "teachable" and welcome part-timers into their departments will the employee culture improve. Second, the brunt falls upon full-timers. Early engagement of full-timers to help train and work in a cooperative way with part-timers is essential. Third, the responsibility falls upon the firm's executives, who must consider the advantages and monitor the process from start to finish. Among other factors, they must monitor the impact of more part-timers on profits, quality of product and service and, ultimately, customer reaction.

SUPERVISING A DIVERSE WORK GROUP

Each department within an organization will have its own cultural and ethnic mix, as well as its own full- and part-time employee work schedule mix. *The efficient use of cultural and work schedule mix is the responsibility of the immediate supervisor.*

What are the major factors that determine the work schedule mix?

1. *Management philosophy.* Most executives strive for high productivity and top quality at the lowest personnel costs. Many with this philosophy lean toward using more part-time employees. But not all.

2. *Financial status.* When some organizations encounter a financial squeeze, they think harder about cutting personnel costs by hiring more part-time employees.

3. *Type of firm.* Service firms with peak periods of customer activity not only favor part-timers, but might not exist without a high percentage of them. Other types of firms must make more of an effort to take advantage of part-time people.

4. *Composition of available work force.* Both the work schedule and cultural mix of a firm will depend upon the local labor pool.

The most important factor is training the immediate supervisor to work with the available personnel. Quality productivity starts and finishes within each department or work team. When the supervisor or team leader has the skills to work with all cultures as well as various work schedules, the organization gets the results and the competitive edge it seeks.

IDEAS AHEAD . . .

DISCOVERING THE BEST MIX

No mix is perfect for all departments within an organization. The occasional exception is when departments (or branches) are so typical that one mix can be prescribed for all.

There are three basic approaches for finding the mix that will lead to the highest performance at the lowest cost.

The Experimental Approach

Each department, section or team experiments with part-timers on various jobs at different time periods. For example, when a full-timer leaves, the immediate questions are: "Will one or more qualified part-timers increase or maintain productivity and cost less? Can the realignment and consolidation of tasks enable one good part-timer to increase productivity and/or reduce cash?"

Whenever you start thinking of changing the work style mix in a given department or section, you, the supervisor, must be deeply involved and, in most cases, make the final decision. The human resource department and its members can and should make recommendations, but ultimately you are responsible for the productivity of your department and the labor costs involved.

The Model Approach

Once a department has done some initial experimenting, a tentative model can be constructed. This model can be shared with both similar and dissimilar departments or teams. When experimentation is going on in more than one department, the human resource department can set up meetings at which to discuss models, make improvements, and share any progress being achieved in one department with others. In smaller firms the owner or manager will have assumed the personnel function. Ultimately, three or more models could be designed and disseminated.

DISCOVERING THE BEST MIX (continued)

The Mandate Approach

Once models have been tried and improved over a substantial period of time, top management might decide to mandate them in similar situations. For example, a branch banking system might design a model that calls for three full-time employees with nine part-timers, and then require branches doing a similar volume of business to use the same mix. Two hypothetical mix opportunities are presented in the case studies that follow. If, through careful analysis, you can come up with a solution, you will have increased your insight into the problems involved.

Case Study: A Flower Shop

Jill and Geraldo operate a highly successful flower shop. Jill has decided that she would like to become a lawyer and leave Geraldo to operate the shop. She would be willing to work part-time on an on-call or emergency basis, especially during holidays.

Currently, the shop employs six full-time and two part-time people. Geraldo hopes to reduce slowly the number of full-timers to two and increase the number of part-timers to ten or twelve. He believes that more talented people will produce more and provide better service at lower costs.

He figures that two assistants can work full time with present benefits—an expensive, comprehensive package. Each assistant can have from five to six part-timers under her or his control. Two part-timers can oversee delivery, one can act as a custodian, and the others can do arranging, serve customers, etc.

How logical is Geraldo's thinking? How long would you estimate it would take him to make such a transition through normal attrition or voluntary change in status? Is he making a smart move? Compare your answer to that of the author, on page 85 in the back of the book.

_____

_____

_____

_____

_____

_____

Case Study: The Chain Operation

You manage a self-service, home-improvement operation which is part of an established chain. Recently, new competition has caused all stores but one to show a reduction in net profit. The owner has called a special meeting of all fourteen store managers to study and analyze labor costs.

An outside consultant has suggested that were the chain to switch to more part-time employees, the cost of labor would be reduced as much as 20 percent. After looking into these costs from all perspectives, the owner asks for volunteers to set up a model mix of full- and part-time employees with a target of lowering labor costs 2 percent on net sales. You and one other manager volunteer.

You currently have sixteen full-time employees, not including two assistant managers. Four of the sixteen are office employees. The rest are involved in sales, stocking and yard work. You decide that you can operate more effectively and at less costs with two full-time and three part-time office employees, and four full-time and fourteen part-timers in sales, stocking and yard work.

Is your model practical? How long would it take to put into practice? What chance would your model have of being adopted throughout the chain? Compare your response with the author's on page 85 in the back of the book.

_____

_____

_____

_____

_____

_____

NOTE: A true model will show (1) the qualities that can be found in part-time applicants, (2) the salary and benefits to be paid, (3) the assignments appropriate for part-timers, (4) impact on sales volume, (5) scheduling chart or matrix, and (6) a new organization chart.

MANAGING FOR COMMITMENT

Think back. Chances are excellent that the first job you ever had was part-time. Perhaps you started out working for a small business owner near your home. Chances are good you still remember her or his name. If you were lucky, the owner became something of a counselor or mentor. If so, you learned a lot, and the owner received a degree of commitment from you. It was a mutually rewarding relationship.

The goal of all supervisors (and small business owners) should be to gain the highest possible commitment from all workers—especially part-timers. How can this best be accomplished? Here are three suggestions.

▶ Convince part-timers that they are building a reputation with you now that will follow them later.

Mario started out as a bus boy in a cafeteria. He was reliable, upbeat and industrious. When he left for college he was an assistant manager, and the manager was pleased to give Mario a letter of recommendation. The letter helped him get a good job near campus.

▶ Let them know that the skills they will learn from you will stand them in good stead in the future.

Salina started out as a stock girl and wound up as a cashier. When she decided to apply for a full-time summer job at a national park, her skills as a fast, accurate, pleasant cashier gave her the edge she needed.

▶ Discuss the possibility that the best thing that can happen in one's first part-time job is to gain personal confidence.

Yasmin finished high school as an honor student, but socially she lagged behind her classmates. Two years later, after working part-time in a fashion boutique while going to college, Yasmin had acquired a personal confidence level to match her academic success.

Most part-timers will commit themselves to a job if they are convinced the experience will enhance their future. It is the job of the supervisor or owner to see that this happens. With commitment comes high productivity, dependability and enthusiasm. Without commitment, the individual is usually an average or below-average employee.

DEVELOP A NEW LEADERSHIP ATTITUDE

With a greater diversity of people, flexible scheduling and more part-timers in their departments, the supervisors of the future need new leadership skills. Here are three suggestions.

1. Go against "traditional" wisdom and demonstrate a more forceful brand of leadership. Be sensitive, but be sure that everyone involved (full-time and part-time) feels the presence of a leader who cannot be denied. To achieve this, the team leader should use the three sources of power, in this order:

Knowledge power: Teaching others to do things right gives you more status among workers.

Personality power: Be a strong, communicative person who has an impact on others.

Role power: If necessary, it is okay to let workers know who is in charge.

2. Create a "force" that energizes those working for you. A work team, similar to a sports team, must be ignited into action. Leadership does this! Rely more on top producers, whether full- or part-time, than the average performers, regardless of their status. Energetic, enthusiastic workers (especially part-timers) can break the traditional pattern of spending fifteen minutes after they clock in getting ready to work, and fifteen minutes getting ready to leave. Add to this the traditional afternoon slump—and it is easy to see why some employers receive only six hours work for eight hours pay. Contrast this to an energetic part-timer who shows up at 1:00 p.m. and works four hours at a high pitch with only one fifteen-minute break. The kind of leadership that seems to create a centrifugal force that motivates workers into reaching their productivity potentials makes good things happen.

3. Make quick definite decisions. Try to involve team members in major decisions where they are involved. But the modern supervisor does not always have time to do this. Decisions usually must be made on the run. To slow down a work tempo to make a decision can be counterproductive. Besides, making fast decisions shows strong, effective leadership. Leaders with this capacity are often heard saying: "Let's do it!" "Get it done!" "Don't drag it out!" "Make it happen!"

To cope with the many changes that are raining on the front-line supervisor, a new, more dynamic form of leadership is required. All workers want to be led—all workers want to feel they are contributing to the goal of higher productivity at a quality level—but the only one who can bring them all together is the team leader.

Eventually, the contribution that part-timers make toward the success of a business will depend upon the leadership of their supervisors.

DEALING EFFECTIVELY WITH ADDED RESPONSIBILITIES

When supervisors first read this manual, many who have gone through quality, productivity and cost-reduction exercises probably will throw up their hands and exclaim: "Upper management is forever sending new responsibilities our way. They eliminate mid-management personnel to become lean and mean, so what happens? Everything falls into the lap of the supervisor. We keep picking up new tasks. Now we must deal with an expanding number of part-timers in addition to the full-timers. How do we come out ahead in a situation like this?"

Such a reaction is natural. The job of the first-line supervisor *has* become more demanding. Some people estimate that so much responsibility has filtered down to the last manager in the hierarchy that the position should be redefined. Some state that the only answer is to give the supervisor more status, authority and training.

The immediate supervisor of the part-time employee must be the one to make any new policy work.

What is the answer?

Better supervisory techniques and solutions!

On the pages that follow, the added responsibilities of using more part-timers are presented as problems (top of page), and possible solutions are discussed (bottom of page). This approach helps prepare supervisors for the extra demands more part-timers will make upon their time.

As you relate to these problems and possible solutions, please keep in mind that every work environment is vastly different from others. It is impossible to prescribe specific techniques that apply equally to, say, a fast-food operation, a bank or an assembly line. These are principles that may or may not apply to the working conditions under which you operate.

CAN YOU SOLVE THESE PROBLEMS?

Strategic Work Force Problem #1

You have decided to expand the number of employees in your small business from twelve full-timers to six full-timers and twelve part-timers. You figure you can save the cost of two full-timers by making this move. You intend to do this slowly as your full-timers retire or leave for other reasons.

You recognize you are creating a few problems for yourself:

- You will have six more employees to deal with.
- Your turnover may be greater with more part-timers.
- Your cultural diversity mix may expand.
- Your age mix may widen.

Are you doing the right thing? Will you lose the stability and predictability of an all-full-time staff? Will the potential savings in labor costs be worth all the additional effort? Will you eventually need to hire another full-timer just to deal with more people?

Possible Solution

If you can find part-time people with the skills you need in your local labor market, you probably are making the right move. The advantages, listed below, should outweigh the disadvantages:

- You will likely be inserting new energy into your staff, with the possibility of reaching higher productivity.
- The blend of one full-timer for every two part-timers should work well.
- The savings in labor costs should enable you to reduce your expenses or to apply them elsewhere in your organization.

Someone will need to retrain full-time employees on how to work better with part-timers. Instead of sitting back (as is often the case) and taking a dim view of part-timers, full-timers will need to help train and motivate the part-timers to be strong team members so they can make a significant contribution to productivity.

Do you agree that full-timers who have shown negative attitudes toward part-timers can be converted into supporters? ❑ **Agree** ❑ **Disagree**

Comments: _____

_____

Strategic Work Force Problem #2

You have worked for the Stark Company for more than thirty years, the last fifteen as a supervisor. You are fifty-eight years old and would like to retire in four years.

In order to survive, your company has initiated a new policy of hiring more part-timers. Accordingly, when Henry retired last year, you replaced him with two part-timers. The arrangement is working rather well. However, they now want you to replace as many as 50 percent (twelve employees) with part-timers. Considering the age of your full-time staff and the attractive early-retirement incentives being offered, you think this will occur in the next two years.

You see many problems:

- Additional flex-scheduling, complicating job assignments.
- More absenteeism, especially among part-timers.
- The need for additional training.
- More problems with people getting along with one another.
- Far more coordination necessary on your part.
- Quality control more difficult to maintain.

You are attending a company seminar on "Team Building," which is designed to help line supervisors work with the new personnel policy. The company's idea is that through team techniques, a more diversified group of employees can be accommodated, productivity will increase and costs will go down.

All of these changes are tempting you to retire now. Should you?

Possible Solution

Consider what you would do with your retirement days. Will you work part-time yourself? Will leaving now reduce your standard of living upon retirement? Also, what about medical protection?

Base your decision upon your attitude toward change. If you are going to resist the changes your company is going to make, early retirement may be best for all concerned. However, try to see how the changes can actually make your job easier.

One is never too old to learn the team approach to supervision. This means learning how to "empower" your employees and place more responsibility on their shoulders. This means training part-timers (both young and experienced) to do a quality job. If you sense you are sufficiently flexible to change your leadership style to fit a less structured team approach to productivity, you could be proud of your ability to make the transition.

The decision should be made 90 percent on the basis of your attitude toward change. ❑ **Agree**   ❑ **Disagree**

Comments: _____

_____

Strategic Work Force Problem #3

You are the training director of a mid-size firm and work directly under the supervision of the director of human resources. Your company has put a freeze on employing full-time employees but, when necessary, permission will be granted to employ part-timers when full-timers retire or resign. You have been asked to develop a two-hour training program for the firm's thirty line supervisors. The program will help supervisors better train new part-time employees.

You decide to build your program around the following three ideas:

1. Every new part-time employee will be assigned a sponsor for the first thirty days on the job. The sponsor will provide all on-the-job training. The supervisor will assign sponsors and monitor their effectiveness. Sponsors will provide one-on-one training on top of their regular job assignments. Either full- or part-time employees may be given this assignment.

2. Supervisors will be encouraged to do some up-front training of their own. That is, they will be asked to hold short, on-the-floor training sessions to upgrade the quality of performance of all employees, including sponsors.

3. Managers will welcome suggestions from supervisors on how the company can recruit and orient new part-timers so they will report on their first assignments better prepared to assume their tasks.

Is this approach appropriate?

Possible Solution

After reviewing your proposed two-hour program, your boss (the director of human resources) wants to add a section giving the supervisors the full financial picture of the firm so that they will understand why there is a freeze on hiring full-timers, how part-timers will reduce costs and why the firm must increase productivity if it is to be competitive. She explains:

> *"I do not believe in scare psychology, but this company is in trouble. The supervisors need to know that it is not business as usual. We must get higher productivity at lower costs or the company is in jeopardy and so are our jobs. I suggest you cover what I am saying during the first hour—furnish facts, what other similar firms are doing—then submit your three-step plan in the second hour."*

Do you agree with the director of human resources? ❑ **Agree**   ❑ **Disagree**

Comments: _____

_____

Strategic Work Force Problem #4

Until a few months ago, you were enthusiastic about your position as a branch manager. You liked the idea of being isolated with little supervision from headquarters, which was located more than fifty miles away. You enjoyed your fourteen full-time and two part-time employees. With two excellent assistants, you had ample time to deal with public relations problems and other responsibilities. You even had time to counsel employees about their personal problems. This was the most enjoyable part of your job.

Now things are increasingly hectic. You are switching to part-time people to save on labor and benefit costs. You have lost one of your assistants. You are dealing with a diversity of pressures that were not evident earlier.

Yesterday, you received a visit from your superior from headquarters. In discussing the many changes and pressures, she said: "Jack, you are trying to operate under an old environment that no longer exists. The tempo has changed, and you won't admit it. We just can't afford full-time employees anymore when we can get part-timers who will work as hard or harder for much less. The only way you and this branch will make a profit in the future is to create a faster tempo."

As you look ahead to the future, you are not so sure you want to be a branch manager. Perhaps you should seek a different career.

Possible Solution

Here are three steps that will help you. First, as you switch to part-timers, make better selections. There are a lot of good people out there seeking part-time jobs. Find them. Second, stay with your successful "team approach" but, as leader, be more direct and business-like. Let it be known that there is time for a little foolishness only after quotas have been reached. And third, let your full-timers know that their jobs are now at a premium and if they expect to keep them over the long haul, they must pick up their productivity.

Do you agree with the suggested steps? Should Jack forget the past and adjust to the changes? ❑ **Agree** ❑ **Disagree**

Comments: _____

_____

Self-Test: Review

What have you learned about part-timers that will help you become a stronger supervisor in the future? To measure your progress, indicate whether you believe the statement is true or false. Correct answers will be found on page 85 at the back of the book.

TRUE   **FALSE**

_____   _____   1. Most organizations can reduce labor costs and increase productivity by the wise use of part-time employees.

_____   _____   2. Part-timers who are ambitious to become full-timers often pressure other employees to produce more.

_____   _____   3. Flex-scheduling is a thing of the past.

_____   _____   4. A "temp" is usually a person who works through an agency but never works on a full-time basis.

_____   _____   5. Part-timers are usually paid less than full-timers, but their benefits are the same.

_____   _____   6. An estimated 20 percent of those in the work force are part-timers.

_____   _____   7. Fewer retirees are interested in part-time work today.

_____   _____   8. In comparison to full-timers, the behavior of part-time workers leaves much to be desired.

_____   _____   9. It is a good idea to give as much attention to the employment of part-timers as full-timers—even if they don't last as long.

_____   _____   10. The goal is productivity, not the number of hours spent on a job.

_____   _____   11. Full-timers are more loyal.

_____   _____   12. The big disadvantage of part-timers is that you can't depend upon them.

TRUE   FALSE

_____   _____   13. This book recognizes that organizations that learn how to work well in the future with part-timers will give themselves a competitive advantage.

_____   _____   14. Factories cannot use part-timers.

_____   _____   15. Customizing full-time jobs is smart; customizing part-time jobs is not.

_____   _____   16. Part-time retirees expect to be given preferential treatment.

_____   _____   17. All departments can benefit from at least one part-time employee.

_____   _____   18. Work teams cannot effectively use part-timers.

_____   _____   19. It is possible to get more productivity per hour from a part-timer than from the average full-timer.

_____   _____   20. The key to the profitable use of a part-timer lies in the hands of the supervisor.

TOTAL CORRECT [   ]

SUMMARY: TEN ACTION STEPS TO TAKE

1. Eliminate any bias you may have toward either full- or part-time employees. A positive attitude toward *all* members of a work team is essential.

2. As you treat all part-timers in a fair and positive manner, keep in mind that all three types of employees (young, experienced and retirees) require special understanding if higher productivity is to be achieved.

3. Accept and adopt the tips on how to get higher productivity from the three types of part-timers.

4. Willingly accept that adjusting work schedules will be more difficult, and concentrate on developing an efficient system. Also, be ready to delegate some of this responsibility to others so you will have free time for other challenges.

5. Become an expert at customizing work assignments for skilled and experienced workers who only want part-time roles. Integrate them into your work teams so that their contribution is maximized.

6. Be receptive to bringing retirees into your department and, if possible, give them assignments where they can make major contributions.

7. Train yourself to use part-timers in such a way as to encourage full-timers to produce more. This may involve using techniques (contests, assignment rotations, etc.) that can only be determined on the spot.

8. Accept the principle that quality productivity is not determined by the length of time spent. An enthusiastic and skillful part-timer can sometimes produce as much or more than a below-average full-timer.

9. Become an expert in interviewing, orienting, training and integrating part-timers of all cultures into your work "team."

10. In your efforts to make better use of part-timers, do not neglect full-timers. Remind yourself that full-timers are the core of your operation and that they should be role models for part-timers.

P A R T

IV

Answers

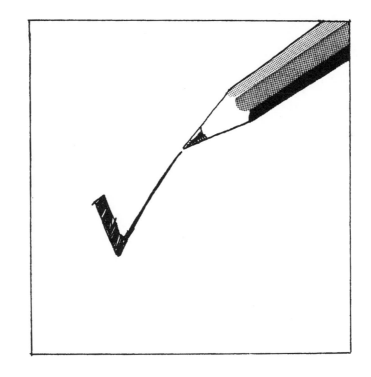

ANSWERS

PART I

Self-Test: Interpretation of Ratings (page 19)

If your ratings are within three points of being equal (either way), you apparently would not prejudge the performance of an employee based upon full- or part-time status; rather, you would evaluate on performance alone.

If you gave five or more excellent ratings to either group, you may have a measurable preference for that type of employee and, as a result, you might not give those from the other group a fair shake.

The tradition of giving preferential treatment to full-time employees remains in many organizations. The forty-hour, full-benefit employee has been accepted as the norm in our work force. Today, with downsizing and restructuring, such unequal treatment must end. Therefore, supervisors must be trained to work more effectively with *all* employees, especially those who work part-time.

PART II

Quiz: Understanding Young Part-Timers (page 45)

1. F (almost but not quite)   **2.** F (most are extremely ready)   **3.** F (they have lived under strict authority figures for too long—they need understanding supervisors who will give them opportunities, not too many rules)
4. T   **5.** T   **6.** F (a little fun creates a team spirit and releases frustration)
7. F (just the opposite)   **8.** F   **9.** T   **10.** T

PART II (continued)

Case Study: Jerry (page 51)

Mr. Barr and his firm stand to benefit the most because Jerry will constitute a one-person research-and-development department. Jerry can work in his own "invention shop" without taking up room in Mr. Barr's plant. No supervision is needed. The cost will be minimal in comparison to the potential benefits. Chances are good that Jerry will either design from scratch or solve design problems in machines already in operation. Moreover, Jerry will have the challenge of working on "real-world" problems without pressure. Although Jerry may not need the additional income, earning and sharing it should give him a feeling of importance. Most essential, the involvement should keep him younger.

Quiz: Understanding Older Part-Timers (page 52)

1. F **2.** T **3.** T **4.** F **5.** T **6.** T **7.** F **8.** F **9.** T **10.** T

Case Study: Jean (page 57)

Jean's chances of getting an organization to customize a job to suit her talents are excellent—especially if she lives in a large community or is willing to commute a sizable distance twice each week. Jean and her husband may have to be more flexible than they appear to be at this point. Some negotiation is usually necessary. It might be best to exclude the words "as a trouble shooter" from the ad.

Case Study: Drake (page 58)

The proposed arrangement between Rick and Drake is promising. Drake could get incoming scripts screened while Rick might be motivated to do better on his own scripts by reading others. Any arrangement that permits both parties to come out ahead is worth a try. The biggest danger is that Rick might try to promote his own scripts instead of working to turn others' into quality possibilities.

Quiz: Job Customization (page 59)

1. F **2.** T **3.** F **4.** T **5.** T **6.** T **7.** T **8.** F **9.** F **10.** F

PART III

Case Study: A Flower Shop (page 67)

The nature of the flower shop operation (slow and peak periods) means that Geraldo's thinking is logical, providing he develops the right kind of working environment for part-timers. Replacing full-time employees with part-timers on an attrition basis might take a number of years. Nevertheless, he is making a smart move. If his productivity increases as his labor costs fall, Geraldo will be able to compete more effectively with chain operations. To make the employee mix work, he will need to be most careful in his selection (interviewing) and training procedures.

Case Study: The Chain Operation (page 68)

The employee mix proposed seems a little out of balance—that is, more than three part-timers for each full-timer may be stretching it too far. But because the transition may take a few years to accomplish, it is always possible to slow down on hiring part-timers. If the model proves that productivity can be increased while labor costs are reduced, it could still be a winner.

Self-Test: Review (page 78)

1. T **2.** T **3.** F **4.** F (temps can be full-time) **5.** F (benefits are usually less) **6.** T **7.** F (it is estimated that more than two million are seeking part-time jobs at any time) **8.** F **9.** T (the better the selection, the longer they last) **10.** T **11.** F (some part-timers are more loyal) **12.** F (the big disadvantage is shorter lengths of employment) **13.** T **14.** F **15.** F **16.** F **17.** F **18.** F (part-timers can become important members of any work team—it is not the number of hours worked that makes a good team member) **19.** T (this is generally true because the part-timer doesn't waste as much time as the typical eight-hour-a-day employee) **20.** T

NOTES

NOTES

NOTES

NOTES

NOTES

NOTES

NOTES

NOTES

NOTES

NOW AVAILABLE FROM CRISP PUBLICATIONS

Books • Videos • CD Roms • Computer-Based Training Products

If you enjoyed this book, we have great news for you. There are over 200 books available in the *50-Minute*™ Series. To request a free full-line catalog, contact your local distributor or Crisp Publications, Inc., 1200 Hamilton Court, Menlo Park, CA 94025. Our toll-free number is 800-442-7477.

Subject Areas Include:

Management

Human Resources

Communication Skills

Personal Development

Marketing/Sales

Organizational Development

Customer Service/Quality

Computer Skills

Small Business and Entrepreneurship

Adult Literacy and Learning

Life Planning and Retirement

CRISP WORLDWIDE DISTRIBUTION

English language books are distributed worldwide. Major international distributors include:

ASIA/PACIFIC

Australia/New Zealand: In Learning, PO Box 1051, Springwood QLD, Brisbane, Australia 4127   Tel: 61-7-3-841-2286, Facsimile: 61-7-3-841-1580
ATTN: Messrs. Gordon

Singapore: 85, Genting Lane, Guan Hua Warehouse Bldng #05-01, Singapore 349569   Tel: 65-749-3389, Facsimile: 65-749-1129
ATTN: Evelyn Lee

Japan: Phoenix Associates Co., LTD., Mizuho Bldng. 3-F, 2-12-2, Kami Osaki, Shinagawa-Ku, Tokyo 141   Tel: 81-33-443-7231, Facsimile: 81-33-443-7640
ATTN: Mr. Peter Owans

CANADA

Reid Publishing, Ltd., Box 69559-109 Thomas Street, Oakville, Ontario Canada L6J 7R4.   Tel: (905) 842-4428, Facsimile: (905) 842-9327
ATTN: Mr. Stanley Reid

Trade Book Stores: *Raincoast Books,* 8680 Cambie Street, Vancouver, B.C., V6P 6M9   Tel: (604) 323-7100, Facsimile: (604) 323-2600
ATTN: Order Desk

EUROPEAN UNION

England: *Flex Training,* Ltd. 9-15 Hitchin Street, Baldock, Hertfordshire, SG7 6A, England   Tel: 44-1-46-289-6000, Facsimile: 44-1-46-289-2417
ATTN: Mr. David Willetts

INDIA

Multi-Media HRD, Pvt., Ltd., National House, Tulloch Road, Appolo Bunder, Bombay, India 400-039   Tel: 91-22-204-2281, Facsimile: 91-22-283-6478
ATTN: Messrs. Aggarwal

SOUTH AMERICA

Mexico: *Grupo Editorial Iberoamerica,* Nebraska 199, Col. Napoles, 03810 Mexico, D.F.   Tel: 525-523-0994, Facsimile: 525-543-1173
ATTN: Señor Nicholas Grepe

SOUTH AFRICA

Alternative Books, Unit A3 Micro Industrial Park, Hammer Avenue, Stridom Park, Randburg, 2194 South Africa   Tel: 27-11-792-7730, Facsimile: 27-11-792-7787
ATTN: Mr. Vernon de Haas